AF488181

For permission requests, write to the publisher, addressed at the address below:
Encore Portfolio LLC
4393 Kevin Walker Suite 1134
Montclair, VA 22193-22025

ISBN 979-8-3302-4885-8

Published in 2025 by Encore Portfolio LLC
Authored by Sharon Sargeant
Editing by Sharon Sargeant and Edward Sargeant

I am happy that you have decided to purchase this guide to help you with your party planning journey. A celebration is a life experience that gives delayed gratification. It's the type of gratification that you want your guests to feel before, during and after the event. These feeling are created when the following happens: smooth transitions, prompt start times, tasty cuisine and great entertainment. I have years of experience planning and organizing many memorable events such as weddings, theme parties, office parties and dinner parties just to name a few. So let's get started planning your memories.

Sharon Sargeant

Disclaimer

The Party Planning Experience is intended to provide creative ideas and general guidance for hosting enjoyable gatherings and celebrations. The author and publisher encourage all readers to plan and host events responsibly and with consideration for the safety and well-being of all guests.

We do not condone underage drinking, illegal activity, reckless behavior, or unsafe practices at any event. Any references to beverages, entertainment, themes, or activities are intended solely for lawful and responsible adult use where permitted by local laws and regulations.

Readers and event hosts are responsible for ensuring that all activities at their events comply with local, state, and federal laws, including laws related to alcohol consumption and guest safety. If alcohol is served at an event, we strongly encourage hosts and guests to drink responsibly, monitor consumption, and provide safe transportation options when necessary.

Additionally, The Party Planning Experience may reference vendors, venues, products, or services that are owned or operated by third parties. The author and publisher do not control or assume responsibility for the actions, policies, or practices of any third-party individuals or organizations that may be mentioned or associated with event planning ideas in this book.

Above all, celebrations should bring people together in a safe, respectful, and enjoyable environment. Hosts are encouraged to create gatherings where all guests feel welcome, comfortable, and protected.

CONTENT

CONTENT

CONTENT

CONTENT

INTRODUCTION TO PARTY PLANNING

This is a comprehensive planning guide to assist anyone who wants to organize a party or celebration. Most celebrations today have a theme, even if it's an office party. These themes can be based on holidays, family-inspired events, milestone birthdays, and more. This guide will lay the foundation for planning your parties. Included is a collection of thematic guides that accompany this planner, focusing on specific party themes and layouts needed for your special day. The key to creating a successful party is organization. By following the steps in this guide, you will experience less stress and be able to enjoy your event. Another important aspect of party planning is seeking assistance. This isn't the type of help usually offered by family and friends, who may prefer to enjoy the party without taking on tasks. Instead, consider hiring additional helpers for the day. For these helpers to be effective, you must first be organized. The ultimate goal is to provide your guests with an experience they will talk about for years to come. So, let's get this party started!

01 ORGANIZATION

Do not skip this section! This is the foundation of everything that will take place in planning the perfect event. This includes the information and instructions needed to take you on your journey. These task will require a binder that you can touch, add pages, and refer to during this process. These items and suggestions will keep you organized.

PLANNER

01

- 1.5" three ring white binder with pockets
- Pens/Pencils
- pencil holder
- Scissors
- Loose leaf paper
- Ruler
- Bag to hold all these items

TIPS

- Make copies of the worksheets that you will need to write on an place them in the binder.
  - vendors, catering, in process and so on.

EMAIL

02

- Create a "Gmail" account
- Use Google Drive
- Create a Pinterest board (see resource area for set-up)

DIGITAL SOFTWARE

03

Familiarize yourself with digital software so that you can communicate fast and easy. This guide suggests using:

- CANVA for invitations and flyers
- ZOOM or Google Meets for video conferencing.
- Cell phone for direct messaging.

THE BUDGET

Planning a successful party involves more than just selecting the perfect theme and inviting guests; it requires careful financial considerations to ensure everything runs smoothly without breaking the bank. Crafting a budget for your party is a crucial first step that lays the foundation for a well-managed and enjoyable event. Whether it's a birthday bash, a holiday gathering, or a special celebration, establishing a realistic budget allows you to allocate resources wisely, prioritize expenses, and prevent any financial surprises along the way. In this guide, we'll explore the essential steps to help you create a comprehensive party budget, ensuring that every aspect of your celebration is memorable.

We have created levels of spending called the party experience. Read and choose the one that fits your personal party planning characteristics and budget. Follow the budget plan for that party experience, and your party is sure to be a success.

01 PLATINUM PARTY EXPERIENCE

The platinum party experience says it all in the title. It is a celebrity style event with all the bells and whistles. After creating a vision, vendors are chosen to execute this plan. You will still need this guide to lay the foundation for your event, however, you have a blueprint with which to complete your tasks. If you choose this party experience, you place your trust in the reviews of the vendors that you choose to create your vision and a day that your guest will remember. Get ready to swipe one of those cards in your wallet, because the price tag on this shindig costs between $10,000 - $15,000.

02 GOLD PARTY EXPERIENCE

The gold party experience is created for those who don't want the stress of completing DIY projects and catering their own food. They don't mind completing some small tasks if it doesn't take up too much time. They like to call vendors to take care of some of the "heavy" areas like catering and decorating. They plan their vision using their Pinterest boards. They like to employ those ideas by modifying them within their budget. This plan will cost between $5000 - $10,000.

03 SILVER PARTY EXPERIENCE

The silver party experience is designed for those who need to plan something quickly and don't want to spend too much money. They aim to execute a champagne plan on a beer budget. This plan relies on many "hands" to assist. The planner will need to adhere closely to the budget and seek free help from friends and family, as well as hire some paid assistance to make it all come together. The cost of this plan ranges between $3,000 and $5,000.

04 BRONZE PARTY EXPERIENCE

The bronze party experience is designed for those who are budget-conscious. By following the same blueprint provided in this book, you can ensure the day runs smoothly. This type of party requires less detailed planning and is suitable for events such as children's parties, family gatherings, small birthday celebrations, Super Bowl parties, holiday get-togethers, dinner parties, or office events. The planner may use their own partyware or shop at discount stores or online for inexpensive disposable options. However, this doesn't mean the party has to look cheap—clever choices can create a polished appearance. The cost of this plan ranges from $1,000 to $3,000.

QUICK REFERENCE
PARTY PLANNING

ITEMS

CAKE

This item can be ordered about 30 days before the event. It should be connected with the theme of the event. There should be an official cake cutter who knows how to cut 1" x 2" slices and how take the layers apart from top to bottom. Use the cake cutting suggestion sheet in this guide or go to YouTube to view cake cutting instructions.

CATERING

If you are planning an event and you have room in the budget to hire a caterer you will need to coordinate that information with the venue (licenses, insurance, etc). Make sure that you purchase enough time for the caterer to set up and break down. They need about an hour before the event and one hour after. You may also use the option of pick-up or drop off catering. Use the worksheets in the guide to coordinate and purchase what is necessary for your catering needs.

DECORATIONS

Once you have decided on a venue and a theme you will be able to determine your décor. If you would like special backdrops or balloon arches you will need to hire a designer. This may take a chunk out of your budget but as the host of this event you will not have time to order a layout and set-up decorations of this magnitude for a party. You cannot blow up balloons, pick up balloons, have your sister pick up the balloons..... Look on Instagram and Facebook for local decorators in your area. Decide what is important for your decor. You may be able to do some small DIY projects. Please look in the resources area for worksheets on this topic. You will thank me for this suggestion later

ENTERTAINMENT

The entertainment segment of the party experience should always have music. Use the planner in the entertainment section to decide on the type of of music and genre that fits you party experience. For example: plan for cocktail hour music using a digital playlist and blue tooth boombox device. For dinner hour plan for live music, if the theme or budget allows and dance the night away with a disc jockey. Visit some of the online websites that have listings of professional disc jockeys or ask your bestie to give recommendations.

RENTALS

The space that you are renting may have some of the items that you will need to complete your space (chairs, tables, bar, etc.). If not you will have to call your local party rental places to get quotes. On occasion, you may want to rent specialty items like bar area, lounge chairs, etc. Place these items on your rental worksheet.

VENUE

The venue for your party is usually half the budget. Some all inclusive venues offer lunch or dinner, and the following items: tables, chairs, table clothes, dishes, centerpieces, audio/visual items, bar and much more. If you need to look for a venue space consider party venue spaces, local clubs, office spaces, firehouses, church halls, lodges, VFWs, Masonic Halls, restaurant spaces and some hotel spaces. Most of these spaces will allow you to bring in an outside caterer. If you choose this type of venue, research your local caterers, a family member or your favorite restaurant for your food menu items.

Platinum
PARTY EXPERIENCE BUDGET

The platinum party experience says it all in the title. It is a celebrity style event with all the bells and whistles. After creating a vision, vendors are chosen to execute this plan. You will still need this guide to lay the foundation for your event, however, you have a blueprint with which to complete your tasks. If you choose this party experience, you place your trust in various vendors to create your vision and a day that your guest will remember. Get ready to swipe one of those cards in your wallet, because the price tag on this shindig costs between $10,000 - $15,000.

PLATINUM BUDGET ITEMS	COST ESTIMATE
Venue/Catering	$6000 - $8,000
Entertainment	$800 - $1000
Photography	$600
Rentals	$300 - $500
Decorations	$1500
Attire	$1000
Dessert/Cake Display	$600
Stationery	0
Bar	$300- $800
Helpers	$500
Contingency	$500
TOTAL	$15,000

Gold
PARTY EXPERIENCE BUDGET

The gold party experience is created for those who don't want the stress of completing DIY projects and catering their own food. They doesn't mind completing some small tasks if it doesn't take up too much time. They like to call vendors to take care of some of the "heavy" areas like catering and decorating. They plan their vision using their Pinterest boards. They like to use those ideas by modifying them within their budget. This plan will cost between $5000 - $10,000.

GOLD BUDGET ITEMS	COST ESTIMATE
Venue/Catering	$4000 - $5500
Entertainment	$500 - $800
Photography	$500
Rentals	$100 - $300
Decorations	$1100
Attire	$500
Dessert/Cake Display	$500
Stationery	0
Bar	$300 - $500
Helpers	$200
Contingency	$100
TOTAL	$10,000

Silver
PARTY EXPERIENCE BUDGET

The silver party experience is created for those who need to plan something quickly and don't want to spend too much money. They want to execute a champagne plan on a beer budget. This plan needs many "hands" to assist. The planner will need to stick closely to the budget and solicit some free assistance from, friends and family members, as well as, and some paid assistance to pull this one off. The cost of this plan ranges between $3000 - $5000.

SILVER BUDGET ITEMS	COST ESTIMATE
Venue/Catering	$1000 - $1500
Entertainment	$300 - $500
Photography	$400
Rentals	$100
Decorations	$600
Attire	$600
Dessert/Cake Display	$500
Stationery	$0
Bar	$100 - $300
helpers	$ 150- $200
Contingency	$300
TOTAL	$5000

*the "$0" for stationery means that this will be digital.

Bronze
PARTY EXPERIENCE BUDGET

This bronze party experience is for the budget conscious. You will follow the same blueprint in this book to make the day run smooth. This party does not need as much detail to plan. Examples of this party experience includes: children's parties, family get-togethers, small birthday parties, superbowl parties, holiday get togethers, , dinner parties or office parties. The planner may use some of their own partyware or go to a discount store or online to purchase inexpensive disposable partyware. This does not mean that it has to look inexpensive. You can fool the eye. This plan will cost between $1000 - $3000.

BRONZE BUDGET ITEMS	COST ESTIMATE
Venue	$0 - $1000
Entertainment	$0
Photography	$200
Rentals	$50 - $200
Decorations	$100 - $300
Attire	$200
Dessert/Cake Display	$200
Catering	$200 - $500
Stationery	$0
Helper	$200
Contingency	$200
TOTAL	$3000

*this plan requires flexibility as noted that some items are "$0". The venue will be "zero" if you are using your home or a free space. This means that you can put these funds under another category. In addition, you may have a friend who can provide entertainment or take professional photographs. The stationery will be digital so this is also "zero". This is a budget friendly plan.

THE PARTY EXPERIENCE BUDGET WORKSHEET

BUDGET ITEMS	COST	NOTES
Venue		
Entertainment		
Photography		
Rentals		
Decorations		
Attire		
Dessert/Cake Display		
Catering		
Stationery		
Helper		
Contingency		
TOTAL		

THE THEME

Since ancient civilizations to the modern era of the 21st Century, platinum events and parties have been planned with purpose and theme. Many parties have a natural theme such as birthday milestones, holidays, and retirements, to name a few. Your guests will treasure enduring memories when you weave a theme throughout every stage of planning. It all commences with the save-the-date or invitation, serving as a gateway to the enchanting moments that lie ahead. Should your venue fail to align with your chosen theme, it can be transformed with décor that envelops guests in a realm where they transcend into the theme once they enter the space. This guide provides the foundation for planning an event with precision and organization in a timely manner. This section offers suggestions for themes for your celebration. Take a look!

THE ULTIMATE PARTY THEME LIST

This is an extensive list of party themes that are popular . Take your time to read through the list of themes. You should visit the Pinterest boards created by The Party Planning Experience.

1 GROWN-UP THEMES

- All Black Affair
- Breakfast at Tiffany's
- Carnival Themed Party
- Casino Night
- Caskers Party (Whiskey)
- Chanel Themed Party
- Cinco De Mayo
- Cooking Class
- Couples Game Night
- Decades (60s, 70s, 80s, 90s)
- Denim and Diamonds
- Derby
- Dorm Room Shower
- Escape Room
- Favorite Things Party
- Gala
- Garden Party
- Graduation
- Grinch Party
- Great Gatsby
- Harlem Nights
- Hawaiian Luau
- House Blessing/Warming
- I Did It My Way
- Karaoke
- Mardi Gras
- Masquerade Ball
- Milestone Birthday
- Military (Promotion | Retirement)
- Monopoly
- Movie Night
- Murder Mystery
- Octoberfest
- Seafood Bowl
- Sneaker Ball
- Sports Team
- Super Bowl
- Sweet Sixteen
- Tea Party
- Waiting to Exhale
- Western Theme Party
- White Party
- Wine Tasting

2 FAMILY THEMES

- Movie Night
- Game Night
- Holiday (Grinch)
- Trivia Night

3 FAMILY REUNION

- African Theme
- Cruise Theme
- Family History/Heritage
- Ski Trip
- Travel Around the World

4 HOLIDAY PARTIES

- Christmas Party
- Christmas Buffet
- Cinco de Mayo
- Easter Dinner
- Friendsgiving Party
- Galentine's
- Halloween ("Boo Bash")
- Juneteenth
- July 4th (Backyard Games)
- Labor Day
- New Year's Eve Party
- Memorial Day Picnic
- St. Patrick's Day Party
- Thanksgiving Buffet
- Valentine's Couples Party

THE ULTIMATE PARTY THEME LIST

5 BABY SHOWER THEMES

- A Little Butterfly in on the way
- A Little Pumpkin is on the way
- A Sweet Little Peanut
- Baby in Bloom
- Boho Chic
- Bun in the Oven
- Ready To Pop
- Safari
- Twinkle, Twinkle Little Star
- We Can Bearly Wait
- Woodland Baby Shower

6 BRIDAL SHOWER THEMES

- Boho Chic
- Breakfast at Tiffany's
- Brunch
- Garden Party
- Lingerie Party
- Love is Brewing
- Love is in Bloom
- Mama Mia She's Getting Married!
- Mexican Fiesta
- Pearls and Prosecco
- Petals and Prosecco
- Pool Party
- Rustic Farmhouse
- She Found Her Honey
- She Found Her Main Squeeze
- She's Fresh Off the Market
- She's Scooped Up (ice cream)
- She's the Wife of the Party
- She's Tying the Knot
- Something Blue Before I Do
- Spa Night
- Summer Beach Bridal Shower
- Tea Party
- The Future Mrs. (Name)
- Travel (Adventure)
- Tropical
- Vintage
- Winery
- Winter Wonderland

7 CHILDREN'S THEME'S

- Animals
- Barbie
- Bluey
- Circus
- Disney Themes
- Dr. Suess
- Enchanted Forest
- Gracie' Corner
- Harry Potter
- Lego
- Marvel Themes
- Minecraft
- Monopoly
- Outer Space
- Pajama Party
- Roblox
- Slumber Party (Tents)
- Spa Party (Spa Truck)
- Super Hero
- Under the Sea
- Unicorn
- Video Game Truck Party

03   THE THEME

MOOD | FLOW | MEMORIES

MOOD

Creating the mood for a party is an art that begins with setting the right atmosphere through lighting, music, and decorations. Start by choosing lighting that complements the theme of the event, whether it's soft and ambient for an intimate gathering or colorful and dynamic for a lively celebration. Select music that not only sets the tone but also encourages guests to engage with the festivities, tailoring the playlist to suit the preferences of the audience. Decorate the space with elements that evoke the desired mood, such as balloons, flowers, or themed props. Consider incorporating scents and aromas to further enhance the ambiance, whether it's with scented candles, fresh flowers, or aromatic diffusers. By carefully curating these elements, you can create a captivating and immersive atmosphere that sets the stage for an unforgettable party experience.

FLOW

A party flows nicely when there is a seamless transition between different activities, ensuring that guests remain engaged and entertained throughout the event. Effective communication between hosts and vendors helps to coordinate timing and logistics, preventing delays or disruptions. Providing ample space for mingling and socializing encourages guests to interact and connect with one another, fostering a lively and inclusive atmosphere. Offering a variety of food and beverage options caters to different tastes and preferences, ensuring that guests are satisfied and engaged. Lastly, having a designated area for activities or entertainment helps to maintain a steady flow of excitement and enjoyment, keeping the party dynamic and memorable.

MEMORIES

Lasting memories at a party are made when guests feel genuinely welcomed and appreciated, fostering a sense of connection and camaraderie. Unique and personalized touches, such as customized decor or interactive activities, leave a lasting impression and make the event memorable. Engaging entertainment that resonates with guests, whether it's live music, games, or performances, creates moments of joy and excitement that they'll cherish long after the party ends. Finally, creating opportunities for meaningful interactions and conversations allows guests to form lasting bonds and memories with one another, ensuring that the party lives on in their hearts and minds.

THEME IDEAS

-
-
-
-
-
-
-
-
-
-
-
-
-
-
-
-
-
-
-
-
-
-
-
-
-
-
-
-
-

TIMELINE

Based on the party experience levels that you learned about in chapter 2 - whether it's platinum, gold, silver, or bronze - you'll be able to seamlessly execute your event using the comprehensive timelines provided on the following pages. These timelines have been carefully crafted to guide you through each stage of party planning, from initial preparations to the big day itself. By adhering to these timelines and dedicating a small amount of time each day to completing tasks, you'll effectively manage your workload and minimize stress as the party date approaches. This structured approach ensures that every aspect of your event receives the attention it deserves, allowing you to focus on creating an unforgettable experience for yourself and your guests.

JAN

S	M	T	W	T	F	S
				1	2	3
4	5	6	7	8	9	10
11	12	13	14	15	16	17
18	19	20	21	22	23	24
25	26	27	28	29	30	31

FEB

S	M	T	W	T	F	S
1	2	3	4	5	6	7
8	9	10	11	12	13	14
15	16	17	18	19	20	21
22	23	24	25	26	27	28

MAR

S	M	T	W	T	F	S
1	2	3	4	5	6	7
8	9	10	11	12	13	14
15	16	17	18	19	20	21
22	23	24	25	26	27	28
29	30	31				

APR

S	M	T	W	T	F	S
		1	2	3	4	
5	6	7	8	9	10	11
12	13	14	15	16	17	18
19	20	21	22	23	24	25
26	27	28	29	30		

MAY

S	M	T	W	T	F	S
				1	2	
3	4	5	6	7	8	9
10	11	12	13	14	15	16
17	18	19	20	21	22	23
24	25	26	27	28	29	30
31						

JUN

S	M	T	W	T	F	S
1	2	3	4	5	6	
7	8	9	10	11	12	13
14	15	16	17	18	19	20
21	22	23	24	25	26	27
28	29	30				

JUL

S	M	T	W	T	F	S
		1	2	3	4	
5	6	7	8	9	10	11
12	13	14	15	16	17	18
19	20	21	22	23	24	25
26	27	28	29	30	31	

AUG

S	M	T	W	T	F	S
					1	
2	3	4	5	6	7	8
9	10	11	12	13	14	15
16	17	18	19	20	21	22
23	24	25	26	27	28	29
30	31					

SEP

S	M	T	W	T	F	S
	1	2	3	4	5	
6	7	8	9	10	11	12
13	14	15	16	17	18	19
20	21	22	23	24	25	26
27	28	29	30			

OCT

S	M	T	W	T	F	S
			1	2	3	
4	5	6	7	8	9	10
11	12	13	14	15	16	17
18	19	20	21	22	23	24
25	26	27	28	29	30	31

NOV

S	M	T	W	T	F	S
1	2	3	4	5	6	7
8	9	10	11	12	13	14
15	16	17	18	19	20	21
22	23	24	25	26	27	28
29	30					

DEC

S	M	T	W	T	F	S
	1	2	3	4	5	
6	7	8	9	10	11	12
13	14	15	16	17	18	19
20	21	22	23	24	25	26
27	28	29	30	31		

JAN

S	M	T	W	T	F	S
					1	2
3	4	5	6	7	8	9
10	11	12	13	14	15	16
17	18	19	20	21	22	23
24	25	26	27	28	29	30
31						

FEB

S	M	T	W	T	F	S
	1	2	3	4	5	6
7	8	9	10	11	12	13
14	15	16	17	18	19	20
21	22	23	24	25	26	27
28						

MAR

S	M	T	W	T	F	S
	1	2	3	4	5	6
7	8	9	10	11	12	13
14	15	16	17	18	19	20
21	22	23	24	25	26	27
28	29	30	31			

APR

S	M	T	W	T	F	S
				1	2	3
4	5	6	7	8	9	10
11	12	13	14	15	16	17
18	19	20	21	22	23	24
25	26	27	28	29	30	

MAY

S	M	T	W	T	F	S
						1
2	3	4	5	6	7	8
9	10	11	12	13	14	15
16	17	18	19	20	21	22
23	24	25	26	27	28	29
30	31					

JUN

S	M	T	W	T	F	S
		1	2	3	4	5
6	7	8	9	10	11	12
13	14	15	16	17	18	19
20	21	22	23	24	25	26
27	28	29	30			

JUL

S	M	T	W	T	F	S
				1	2	3
4	5	6	7	8	9	10
11	12	13	14	15	16	17
18	19	20	21	22	23	24
25	26	27	28	29	30	31

AUG

S	M	T	W	T	F	S
1	2	3	4	5	6	7
8	9	10	11	12	13	14
15	16	17	18	19	20	21
22	23	24	25	26	27	28
29	30	31				

SEP

S	M	T	W	T	F	S
			1	2	3	4
5	6	7	8	9	10	11
12	13	14	15	16	17	18
19	20	21	22	23	24	25
26	27	28	29	30		

OCT

S	M	T	W	T	F	S
					1	2
3	4	5	6	7	8	9
10	11	12	13	14	15	16
17	18	19	20	21	22	23
24	25	26	27	28	29	30
31						

NOV

S	M	T	W	T	F	S
	1	2	3	4	5	6
7	8	9	10	11	12	13
14	15	16	17	18	19	20
21	22	23	24	25	26	27
28	29	30				

DEC

S	M	T	W	T	F	S
			1	2	3	4
5	6	7	8	9	10	11
12	13	14	15	16	17	18
19	20	21	22	23	24	25
26	27	28	29	30	31	

PLANNING CALENDAR

SUN	MON	TUE	WED	THU	FRI	SAT

PLANNING CALENDAR

<table>
<tr><td>SAT</td><td></td><td></td><td></td><td></td><td></td></tr>
<tr><td>FRI</td><td></td><td></td><td></td><td></td><td></td></tr>
<tr><td>THU</td><td></td><td></td><td></td><td></td><td></td></tr>
<tr><td>WED</td><td></td><td></td><td></td><td></td><td></td></tr>
<tr><td>TUE</td><td></td><td></td><td></td><td></td><td></td></tr>
<tr><td>MON</td><td></td><td></td><td></td><td></td><td></td></tr>
<tr><td>SUN</td><td></td><td></td><td></td><td></td><td></td></tr>
</table>

SIX WEEK PLAN

WEEK ONE
01

Party Planning

Budget

Theme

Timeline

WEEK TWO
02

Vendors

Guest List

Save-the-Date

Entertainment

WEEK THREE
03

Decorations

Attire

Meeting of the Minds

WEEK FOUR
04

Invitation

Entertainment

Seating Chart

Shopping List

WEEK FIVE
05

Party Assistants

Party Coordinator

Fine Tune

WEEK SIX
06

Day Before/Day Of Planning

It's Party Time!

After the Party

*if you need to plan a quick party in about three weeks combine tasks (e.g., week one 01-02; week two 03-04 and so on; Text me I will assist).

TIMELINE
WEEK ONE

01 INTRODUCTION TO PARTY PLANNING

Complete everything in chapter 1 to lay the foundation for weeks to come.

02 BUDGET

Choose a budget that fits your available funds and follow that format to begin creating your party plan. Use the "1 Free consultation call to get started",

03 THEME

Once you have chosen a theme begin ordering items and placing those items in a box.

04 TIMELINE

Follow this timeline to make sure you are completing this so that you don't get overwhelmed. If you plan to create some type of photo slideshow or digital movie, now is the time to plan for that. Create a rough draft of a program for the party. This will assists with time management.

TIMELINE
WEEK TWO

01 GUEST LIST

Begin completing this task in week two of the planning phase. Follow the instructions in chapter 5. It will make life much easier.

02 VENDORS

Begin this list with deciding on a venue. If this is not a free space you will need to secure a space large enough to accommodate your theme and guest count. In addition, you need to consider the catering, entertainment and hotel accommodations if needed. This is a heavy time-on-task activity.

03 SAVE THE DATE

Once you have secured your venue, you will be able to send out your first text of correspondence. This is the save the date digital document that you, a friend you assign or a coordinator can text using the list that you created during the first part of the week. Make sure you write legibly so that they can read the names and numbers.

04 ENTERTAINMENT

There are many facets of entertainment to be had, however, the number one area that keeps the mood alive is music. Once you have completed the other tasks for the program you may want to splurge on this part of the entertainment if you have funds left in the budget.

TIMELINE
WEEK THREE

01 DECORATIONS

Now that you have figured out a venue its time to decide on the décor that will be needed for your theme.   Use the worksheets to plan each area that you will need decorations. If you are using a vendor use the worksheet to share your vision. Send photos of the venue to help with create the look that you are going for.

02 ATTIRE

Every themed party needs a special outfit. Begin shopping for those special signature pieces at your grand affairs boutique, local thrift store, online store, or local party store.

03 PRINT ITEMS

If you are planning to have items printed to place in your venue such as: banners, napkins, special glasses, programs, menu cards, drink menus, etc. Now is the time to find those vendors and order those items. If you are creating them on Canva begin working on the digital items and prepare for printing at your local print stores.

04 MEETING OF THE MINDS

During this week take some time to put together a dream team to assist with tasks that will needed to make this day run smooth.   Set a time that everyone can have uninterrupted time on Google Meets or Zoom. Create an agenda and text it to them before the meeting. You will create a "live" to do list to refer to while going through the party planning process.

TIMELINE
WEEK FOUR

01 INVITATION

Invitations - You will be designing a digital product to text to all your guests. Use the verbage in the digital communication area to pair with this type of invitation, because you will need a text response back from your guests.

02 ENTERTAINMENT

Begin creating and fine tuning your digital playlist if you are using this format for music. Make sure that all of you entertainment vendors are locked in.

03 SEATING CHART

You will create a digital card to text to your guest three days before the event. If you have a contingency amount left in your budget a chart with names and table numbers would look nice. Remember this will require an easel, poster (Staples) and time to create it. Create a matching set (table number and chart). You can find templates on Etsy so that you don't have to reinvent the wheel.

04 SHOPPING LIST

You will need to use the "IN PROCESS" worksheet to complete a grocery shopping list if you are purchasing food. In addition, create other lists that you may need using this worksheet.

TIMELINE
WEEK FIVE

01 PARTY ASSISTANT

You will need 1 to 2 party assistants to help with extra duties. Based on your budget this could be a family member or friend. The budget is set to hire an assistant for $25-$40 and hour. There is a task sheet in this guide in the resource section with suggestions on how they can assist for the day (bartender, cake cutter, decorations, coat check, clean up). Respect their time and value that they bring to your party planning experience. Don't forget to bless them with a tip.

02 PARTY COORDINATOR

This person will assist with keeping everything running smooth according to the timeline that you have created. This coordinator can be a family member, friend or hired help. This task should be delegated to someone who understands how to complete this task.

03 FINE TUNE

Fine Tune All Areas - You will need to go over all areas and items that are needed to make the day run smoothly. The people who have agreed to assist will need to be updated. This would be a good time to have a Zoom Meeting. Don't stress about things that are not important. If you have not done them and they are not important to the function of the party forget about it. This will cause unnecessary stress.

TIMELINE
WEEK SIX

01 DAY BEFORE/DAY OF PLANNING

Update and confirm information with everyone involved in your party planning experience. Complete your worksheets.

- guest
- vendors (ALL)
- entertainment
- day of planner
- party assistants
- decorator
- logististics

02 IT'S PARTY TIME!

Use the checklist in this guide to check it once, and check it twice so that you don't forget anything. Pack your party items the night before and place in a strategic location. Plan ahead.

03 AFTER THE PARTY

- send a thank you note to your guest
- send a specific "Thank You" to those gift givers
- share photos
- start thinking about planning the next bash!

04 | THE TIMELINE PARTY EXPERIENCE

THREE MONTH PLAN

MONTH ONE

01

Party Planning
Budget
Theme
Timeline
Vendors
Guest List

MONTH TWO

02

Save-the-Date
Vendors
Decorations
Attire
Entertainment
Meeting of the Minds

MONTH THREE

03

Invitation
Day Before/Day Of Planning
Seating Chart
Party Assistants
Fine Tune All Areas
It's Party Time!
After the Party

TIMELINE MONTH ONE

01 INTRODUCTION TO PARTY PLANNING

Complete everything in chapter 1 to lay the foundation for weeks to come.

02 BUDGET

Choose a budget that fits your available funds and follow that format to begin creating your party plan. Use the "1 Free consultation call to get started",

03 THEME

Once you have chosen a theme begin ordering items and placing those items in a box.

04 TIMELINE

Follow this timeline to make sure you are completing this so that you don't get overwhelmed. If you plan to create some type of photo slideshow or digital movie, now is the time to plan for that. Create a rough draft of a program for the party. This will assists with time management.

05 VENDORS

Begin this list with deciding on a venue. If this is not a free space you will need to secure a space large enough to accommodate your theme and guest count. In addition, you need to consider the catering, entertainment and many other components. This is a heavy time-on-task activity.

06 GUEST LIST

Begin completing this task in week two of the planning phase. Follow the instructions in chapter on guest list. It will make life much easier.

TIMELINE
MONTH TWO

01 SAVE THE DATE

Once you have secured your venue, you will be able to send out your first text of correspondence. This is the save the date digital document that you, a friend you assign or a coordinator can text using the list that you created during the first part of the week. Make sure you write legibly so that they can read the names and numbers.

03 DECORATIONS

Once you have secured your venue, you will be able to send out your first text of correspondence. This is the save the date digital document that you, a friend you assign or a coordinator can text using the list that you created during the first part of the week. Make sure you write legibly so that they can read the names and numbers.

05 ENTERTAINMENT

Continue making connections with your entertainment vendors if you have hired any. Also continue to fine tune any digital playlist that will be needed.

02 VENDORS

Begin this list with deciding on a venue. If this is not a free space you will need to secure a space large enough to accommodate your theme and guest count. In addition, you need to consider the catering, entertainment and hotel accommodations if needed. This is a heavy time-on-task activity.

04 ATTIRE

There are many facets of entertainment to be had, however, the number one area that keeps the mood alive is music. Once you have completed the other task for the program you may want to splurge on this part of the entertainment if you have funds left in the budget.

06 MEETING OF THE MINDS

During this week take some time to put together a dream team to assist with tasks that will needed to make this day run smooth. Set a time that everyone can have uninterrupted time on Google Meets or Zoom. Create an agenda and test it to them before the meet. You will create a "live" to do list to refer to while going through the party planning process.

04 TIMELINE MONTH THREE

01 INVITATION

Invitations - You will be designing a digital product to text to all your guests. Use the verbage in the digital communication area to pair with this type of invitation, because you will need a text response back from your guests.

03 PARTY ASSISTANTS

You will need 1 to 2 party assistants to help with extra duties. Based on your budget this could be a family member or friend. The budget is set to hire an assistant for $25-$40 and hour. There is a task sheet in this guide in the resource section with suggestions on how they can assist for the day (bartender, cake cutter, decorations, coat check, clean up). Respect their time and value that they bring to your party planning experience. Don't forget to bless them with a tip.

05 IT'S TIME TO PARTY!

Use the checklist in this guide to check it once, and check it twice so that you don't forget anything. Pack your party items the night before and place in a strategic location. Plan ahead.

02 DAY BEFORE/DAY OF PLANNING

Update and confirm information with everyone involved in your party planning experience. Complete your worksheets.

- guest
- vendors (ALL)
- entertainment
- day of planner
- party assistants
- decorator

04 FINE TUNE ALL AREAS

Fine Tune All Areas - You will need to go over all areas and items that need to make the day run smoothly.

06 SEATING CHART

You will create a digital card to text to your guest three days before the event. If you have a contingency amount left in your budget a chart with names and table numbers would look nice. Remember this will require an easel, poster (Staples) and time to create it. Create a matching set (table number and chart). You can find templates on Etsy so that you don't have to reinvent the wheel.

THE GUEST LIST

Whether you have 10 guests or 500 guests creating this list is a daunting task. However, once you get all the names and phone numbers of your guests you will feel like you have accomplished a big goal. The philosophy of this guide is built on saving time. Since all of our friends have cell phones its best to create digital correspondence.

You will need to follow the instructions for creating the party list. If you decide to pass this task one to you social media coordinator (or friend) you will have this document with all of the numbers and information to scan and email it to them. The digital age is wonderful. It saves so much time. However, if you would like to add the elegance of a mailed invitation you will need to collect addresses from each of your guests. A great way to complete this task is by having them complete a Google form. If you are not tech savvy have a friend to assist with this task.

Follow the steps below to began creating a guest list . . .
- Begin to create a party list. Use the worksheet on the pages provided to jot down names and phone numbers in pencil.
- This form will be used to text your digital items (save-the-date, invitation, hotel information, table numbers, thank you cards, directions, etc.).
- When you have completed this go to the digital communication chapter to complete your digital tasks.

You may need to call some guests who are not tech savvy like mothers, aunties, and grandmothers (those who may not be social media users) and ask for their information over the phone.

THE GUEST LIST

GATHERING GUESTS INFORMATION
ESTIMATED GUEST COUNT ________

FOLLOW THE STEPS BELOW

- Start by creating a list of family members, friends, and co-workers. Use the worksheet on the following pages to write down the names of guests you would like to invite (in pencil). This list will serve as a rough draft to help you gather the information needed for the formal invitations and correspondence you will send to those attending event.
- Next, you will need to create a Google Form with this information:
  - Title (Ms. Mr., Mrs., Dr., Drs. Honorable),
  - First Name
  - Last Name
  - Address
  - City
  - State (Two Letters)
  - Zip
  - phone number
  - email (optional)

- If you are not tech savvy, you can visit Youtube to search for instructions on "HOW TO CREATE A GOOGLE FORM"
- This Google Form will capture the information and place it in a spreadsheet for you to manipulate during the entire process.
- You will need to create a short link to text to invited guest. This information is located at the top of the Google form.
- First, text a friend with the message below and the short google form link to see if all things are working properly.
- If everything is working as planned, text those people that you have on your list with the message below.

You may need to call some guests who are not tech savvy like mothers, aunties, grandmothers (those who may not be social media users) and ask for their information over the phone. Complete the form for them so that all information will be in one place.

SAMPLE

"I am planning (event: Baby Shower, Milestone Birthday Party).
In preparation for this event, I have begun gathering information
for my special invited guests. I would be honored with your presence
at my (event). Please complete the form provided by clicking the
link in this text."

GUEST LIST

NO.	NAME	PHONE NUMBER
1		
2		
3		
4		
5		
6		
7		
8		
9		
10		
11		
12		
13		
14		
15		

GUEST LIST

NO.	NAME	PHONE NUMBER
16		
17		
18		
19		
20		
21		
22		
23		
24		
25		
26		
27		
28		
29		
30		

GUEST LIST

NO.	NAME	PHONE NUMBER
31		
32		
33		
34		
35		
36		
37		
38		
39		
40		
41		
42		
43		
44		
45		

GUEST LIST

NO.	NAME	PHONE NUMBER
46		
47		
48		
49		
50		
51		
52		
53		
54		
55		
56		
57		
58		
59		
60		

GUEST LIST

NO.	NAME	PHONE NUMBER

THE VENDORS

Coordinating vendors for your party is paramount to ensuring a seamless and successful event. This coordination allows for a cohesive experience where every aspect of the event, from decorations to entertainment, aligns seamlessly with your desired theme and atmosphere. If you follow the steps in this section, you can ensure that your party will reflect your vision and create a memorable experience for your guests.

Following this guide will also prevent overlaps or gaps in services, ensuring that each vendor knows their role and schedule within the event timeline. This means that the caterer won't arrive before the venue is set up. It means that the entertainment will start as the guests arrive to set the mood of the party. With proper coordination, potential conflicts or logistical challenges can be identified and resolved proactively, minimizing disruptions and enhancing the overall flow of the event.

FINDING A VENDOR

Online Research

Using online research and directories is a great way to find vendors in your area of the county. Websites like Yelp and Google Maps, or specialized event planning platforms can help you discover vendors based on their proximity to your location. They usually have pictures and reviews to help you make optimum choices.

Social Media

Don't just scroll your favorite social media platform to find out the latest gossip. Check platforms like Facebook, Instagram, or LinkedIn for local vendor groups or pages. These platforms often have communities where vendors advertise their services and where you can find reviews and recommendations from previous clients.

Recommendations

Reach out to friends, family, colleagues or neighbors who have recently organized similar events. They may be able to recommend vendors they've worked with and trust.

SECURING A QUOTE

Schedule a Meeting/Consultation

Reach out to your selected vendors to schedule meetings or consultations. Use this opportunity to discuss your event details, ask questions, and get a sense of their professionalism and responsiveness. Use the worksheets provided to jot down important information that they give and ask questions.

Request Quotes and Proposals

After meeting with vendors, request quotes or proposals outlining their services, pricing, and any additional fees. Compare these offerings to determine which vendors align best with your budget and vision for the event.

Check References

Don't hesitate to ask vendors for references from previous clients. Contact these references to inquire about their experiences working with the vendor and any feedback they may have.

Secure Contracts

Once you've selected your preferred vendors, finalize the details of your agreements and secure contracts outlining the terms and conditions of their services, including payment schedules, cancellation policies, and deliverables.

06 | THE VENUE RENTAL EXPERIENCE

Use the worksheet below to write down the names of venues that you plan to call or email.

- Once you have made a choice on which venue to call, collect needed information below.
- Ask questions that you may have about food choices, how it is packaged and if they offer delivery or if they offer set up.
- Get a contact name, contract, sign it and place it in your party planning experience portfolio.
- Connect with the venue as you get closer to the event date to confirm your date, time of deliveries and payment arrangements.

NO. OF GUESTS _______________

VENUE	INFORMATION
PRICE/QUOTE	
PHONE	
EMAIL	
NOTES	

VENUE	INFORMATION
PRICE/QUOTE	
PHONE	
EMAIL	
NOTES	

CHOOSE A FOOD VENDOR

Many party planners have a small business caterer in mind or have been given recommendations. By all means support those small businesses. Below you will find a list of options that can be used to satisfy the food vendor option. This is a list of some of your neighborhood restaurants that may be located in your area of the county. These restaurants cater large quantities of food. Call or go online to get a quote. Also check ezcater.com.

- Boston Market
- Buffet (any buffet place near you)
- Capital Grill
- Carabbas Italian Restaurant
- Cheesecake Factory
- Chipotle
- Church's Chicken
- Famous Dave's
- Golden Corral
- Hooters
- Jersey Mike's
- KFC
- Maggiano's Little Italy
- Mission Barbeque
- Olive Garden
- On the Border
- Panda Express
- Panera Bread
- Popeyes
- Red Robin
- PF Chang
- Ruth's Chris Steak House
- Subway
- Texas Roadhouse

INFORMATION

When you call these places you should have the following research finished.

- go on their website to view their selections
- know your guest count
- have a menu selection in mind
- have your "in process" worksheet to write down important information

  - appetizers
  - entrée (s)
  - starch
  - vegetable
  - bread
  - dessert

TIPS

- consider ordering appetizers from one of these restaurants to save time
- to cut cost, you can order entrees online and make sides at home
- to cut cost you can get bread from Costo or your local grocery store
- you can purchase gallons of tea/lemonade from the grocery store if you do not want to make it
- follow the checklist provided in the resources section of this guide

06 | THE CATERING EXPERIENCE

Use the worksheet below to write down the names of caterers that you plan to call or email.

- Once you have made a choice on which caterer to call, collect needed information below.
- Ask questions that you may have about food choices, how it is packaged and if they offer delivery or if they offer set up.
- Get a contact name, contract, sign it and place it in your party planning experience portfolio.
- Connect with the caterer as you get closer to the event date to confirm your date, time of deliveries and payment arrangements.

NO. OF GUESTS _______________

CATERER	COST ESTIMATE
PRICE/QUOTE	
PHONE	
EMAIL	
NOTES	

CATERER	COST ESTIMATE
PRICE/QUOTE	
PHONE	
EMAIL	
NOTES	

 THE CATERING EXPERIENCE

This part of the party planning experience is like being in your kitchen, which is the heart of the home. Everyone wants to come in and enjoy good food and drink. "Oh, the food was so delicious". These are the words that you want your guest to say at the end of the celebration. If you are not renting a place that caters the food, you will need to prepare your own food space and choose a food vendor. You will also need to solicit some assistance with logistics of receiving the food and having it served if you don't want everyone just dipping in and taking more than they need. The following pages have a suggested menu for a small party. Use the list below and expand it, to set up your own catering station.

ITEMS

UTENSILS	TABLE SETTING	MENU

• portable chafing dish serving sets
• one per dish
• sterno
• foil
• serving utensils
• condiments (salt, pepper, butter, hot sauce, tartar sauce, salad dressings
	• plates (dinner, salad, and dessert)
	• clear cups
	• forks, knives, spoons
	• napkins
		• Entrée(s) 1 to 2
		• starch
		• vegetable
		• bread
		• garden salad
		• tea/water
		• ice cream or sorbet/cake
		• There are many of your favorite restaurants that cater large quantities
		• Think of planning something that is basic: SAMPLE
		  ○ chicken/salmon
		  ○ rice or potato
		  ○ vegetable
		  ○ rolls
		  ○ garden salad (two dressings)
		  ○ make a sorbet for dessert

TIPS

- purchase a plastic container and use a cart with wheels to move heavy items.
- pack ALL items in bags and place near the door that your will go out of for the party
- purchase bags from Marshall's or TJMaxx because they are strong with handles
- cut up your lemons and limes the night before and place in a sandwich bag
- purchase a discount store shoe box to place the small items in so that you can find them (place packing tape on each end so that items do not spill out during travel)
- give your helpers the instruction sheet provided so that they know what to do when they arrive

THE CATERING EXPERIENCE

This is a sample chart to show you how to organize and plan your buffet table. There is a blank worksheet in the resource area to assist with assembling your buffet. Your buffet line should be set up in a manner that allows guests to move without interruption. The drinks and desserts should be at a separate station.

ITEMS	SERVING DISH CONTAINER	UTENSILS
CHICKEN	CHAFING DISH SET	TONGS
SALMON	CHAFING DISH SET	TONGS
RICE	CHAFING DISH SET	SPOON
STRINGS BEANS	CHAFING DISH SET	SPOON
GARDEN SALAD	BOWL	TONGS
ROLLS	BASKET	TONGS
UTENSILS	CADDY	----
PLATES/NAPKINS	ON TABLE	----

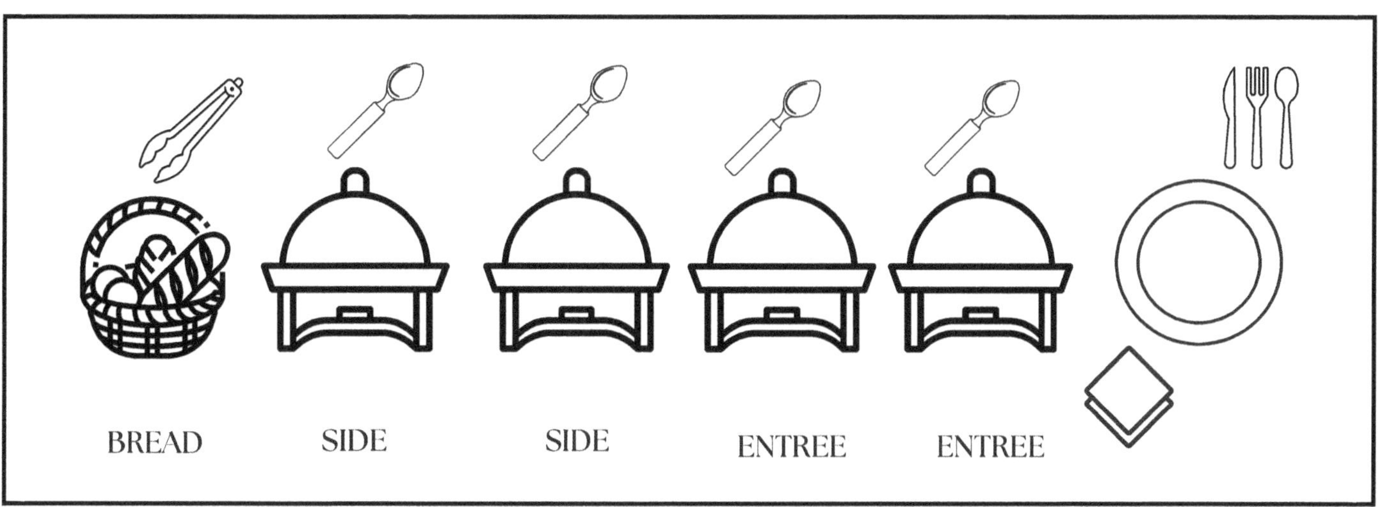

MENU #1 BAKED CHICKEN (30 PEOPLE)	ESTIMATE
ENTREE #1 - CHICKEN	
• frozen breast (boneless) Get a recipe from Youtube or (Aldi Garlic and Herb Frozen chicken breast about 7 pieces of chicken come in a bag (7 bags @$7.98)	$55.86
SIDE DISH - RICE	
• Earthly Grain Long Grain and Wild Rice (12 boxes @ 2.19)	$26.28
SALAD (LETTUCE, CUCUMBER, TOMATO, RANCH AND BALSAMIC DRESSING)	
• 2 (16 oz lettuce containers) 1 (8 oz lettuce container) • 18 roma tomatoes (4 slices on each salad) • baby cucumbers (5 slices on each salad) • shreaded carrots for color • salad dressing (ranch and balsamic vinegar)	$45.00
VEGETABLE (STRING BEANS)	
• Tradeer Joe's Extra Fine String Beans (12 bags @ $1.99) • Butter - Land-O-Lakes (1 lb @ $5.98) • Herbs - garlic powder, salt , pepper and fresh parsley ($3.00)	$33.00
BREAD (HAWAIIAN ROLLS -24 rolls (3 @ $7.66)	$22.98
• 1 box Lipton/2 bags of sugar/10 lemons/3 bags of ice/5- 1 gallon jugs of water (to hold the tea after you make it the night before)	$20.00
TOTAL	$203.12

In order to make this catering choice work within budget you will need to shop at Aldi or Walmart in your area of the county.

MENU #2 CHINESE FOOD (30 PEOPLE)	ESTIMATE
ENTREES (CHOOSE TWO)- CHINESE FOOD	
• Beef with Mixed Chinese Vegetables/Chicken Fried Rice • (10 containers @$12.00)	$120.00
SALAD (Lettuce, cucumber, tomato, ranch and balsamic dressing) • 2 (16 oz lettuce containers) 1 (8 oz lettuce container) • 18 roma tomatoes (4 slices on each salad) • baby cucumbers (5 slices on each salad)	$36.00
VEGETABLE (STRING BEANS)	
• Trader Joe's Extra Fine String Beans (12 bags @ $1.99) • Butter - Land-O-Lakes (1 lb @ $5.98) • Herbs - chopped garlic , salt , pepper and fresh parsley ($3.00)	$33.00
BREAD (HAWAIIAN ROLLS - 24 rolls (3 @ $7.66)	$22.98
• 1 box Lipton/2 bags of sugar/10 lemons/3 bags of ice/5- 1 gallon jugs of water (to hold the tea after you make it the night before)	$20.00
TOTAL	$231.98

In order to make this catering choice work within budget you will need to visit your favorite Chinese place and discuss what you are trying to do. Don't tell them that it is for a catering. Most of the time when you order Chinese food entrée containers, they usually feed 4-6 people(with other items on the plate). A family member or bestie will need to assist with plating and servicing the food.

This is a signature space at your party. You will get a "round of applause" if you have what your guest like to drink. You should begin collecting these items early so that you are not running from store to store looking for specific items. This list was created for those who have a rented or home venue. Someone will need to be hired to cover this station. This alcohol list was created with people's favorite drinks in mind. This guide includes a signature drink "batch mix" menu for two popular drinks.

ITEMS

BAR UTENSILS	ALCOHOL	MIXERS

• shaker (2)
• wipes
• ice bucket and tongs
• coolers (2)
• knife
• wine opener
• bottle opener
• bar napkins
• long toothpicks
• wine stoppers
• bar straws (small glass for them)
• drink dispenser (2.5 gallons)
• clear cups 9 oz
  ○ 20 ppl - 30 - 40
  ○ 40 ppl - 50 - 60
• sandwich bags
• scissors
• 6 ft rectangle table
• stretch black tablecloth
	• Bacardi Rum (1)
	• Hennessy VS Cognac (1)
	• Tito's Vodka (1)
	• Patron (1)
	• Crown Royal (1)
	• Gin (1)
	• Wine
	  ○ white, rose, red
	• Prosecco Champagne
	• beer
		• cokes (12- cans)
		• ginger ale (12 cans)
		• Pineapple juice
		• Lemon Juice
		• Simply Lemonade
		• Orange Juice
		• Sweet and Sour Mix
		• cranberry cocktail
		
		• bags of ice 7lb
		  ○ 20 ppl - 6
		  ○ 40 ppl - 8
		• garnish - cherries, lemons, limes

TIPS

- purchase a plastic container and use a cart with wheels to move these heavy items.
- cut up your lemons and limes the night before and place in a sandwich bag
- pack all of your items in the containers and place them near the door
- purchase a discount store shoe box to place the small items in, so that you can find them (place packing tape on each end so that items do not spill out during travel)
- if the space does not have a bar area you will need the suggested 6ft table and stretch tablecloth

This page includes two signature drinks (batch mix). Your "batch drink" should fit the theme of your party. Guest are "wowed" by the special formula of a "big batch drink". This type of drink alleviates the thought process of what to order at the bar. Some of these drinks can be created a day ahead and placed in the refrigerator.

SIGNATURE "BIG BATCH DRINKS"

Bourbon Peach Lemonade Punch	White Grape Sangria
(can be made the day before the event)	(make the morning of the event)

Bourbon Peach Lemonade Punch

6 c. of sugar
2 c. of water
2 large lemons
64 oz. of Simply Lemonade
1 bag of frozen peaches (thawed)
1 small bunch of mint
1 (750ml) of Whiskey
2- 1 gallon containers of water (you will pour out the water and use this to hold the signature drink)

White Grape Sangria

2 containers of white grape juice
1 (750) ml of Bacardi Rum
1 bottle of Riesling
1 liter sparkling water
2 - honey crisp apples
1 - orange
2 large lemons
2- 1 gallon containers of water (you will pour out the water and use this to hold the signature drink)

Directions

- Combine water and sugar in a microwave safe bowl or glass measuring cup and microwave on high for 2 minutes or until water is hot to make simple syrup. Stir until sugar is dissolved. You can also heat the water and sugar in a saucepan over medium-high heat until sugar is dissolved.
- Squeeze the juice from the lemons and place in large container. Pour sugar water into a pitcher along with lemon juice. Muddle and mash the peaches, and add the bourbon. Chop a few of the mint leaves and add to taste. Pour into the gallon jugs and refrigerate overnight or until ready to serve.

Directions

- Squeeze the juice from the lemons and place in a large container. Slice apples and oranges and place in bowl. Pour the container of white grape juice, 1/2 bottle of Riesling, 1/2 liter sparling water and 1/2 bottle of rum. Stir with a big spoon.
- Pour this batch into one of the gallon jugs after pouring out the water and refrigerate overnight or until ready to serve. REPEAT
- Serve over crushed ice and garnish with lemon and cherry (on a toothpick).

06 | THE BAKERY EXPERIENCE

Use the worksheet below to write down the names of bakeries that you plan to call or email. Use the following page to sketch a theme or print and paste your ideas on this page.

- Once you have made a choice on which bakery to call, take down information about that during the conversation.
- Ask questions that you may have about theme types, cake sizes, flavors and icing, how it is packaged and if they offer delivery or if they offer set up.
- Get a contact name, contract, sign it and place it in your party planning experience portfolio.
- Connect with the bakery as you get closer to the event date to confirm your date, time of delivery or pick up and payment arrangements.

NO. OF GUESTS ————————————————

BAKERY	INFORMATION
PRICE/QUOTE	
PHONE	
EMAIL	
NOTES	

BAKERY	INFORMATION
PRICE/QUOTE	
PHONE	
EMAIL	
NOTES	

BAKERY

DESIGN YOUR CAKE

CAKE CUTTING INSTRUCTIONS

SHEET CAKES	
CAKE	GUESTS
12 x 12	70
9 x 13	52
12 x 18	52
14 x 22	152

ROUND CAKES	
CAKE	GUESTS
6 inch round	8
8 inch round	14
10 inch round	20
12 inch round	26
14 inch round	40

SQUARE CAKES	
CAKE	GUESTS
6 inch square	9
8 inch square	16
10 inch square	24
12 inch square	34
14 inch square	48

these estimates are based on cutting a 1" x 2" piece of cake

06 | THE DECORATING EXPERIENCE

Use the worksheet below to write down the names of party designers that you plan to call or email.

- Once you have made a choice of which decorators to call, collect needed information below
- Ask questions that you may have about their timeline, types of set up for your venue, appointments to look at the venue, etc.
- Get a contact name, contract, sign it and place it in your party planning experience portfolio.
- Connect with the decorator as you get closer to the event date to confirm your date, timeline and final payment arrangements.

NO. OF GUESTS _______________

DECORATOR	INFORMATION
PRICE/QUOTE	
PHONE	
EMAIL	
NOTES	

DECORATOR	INFORMATION
PRICE/QUOTE	
PHONE	
EMAIL	
NOTES	

06 DECORATING LIST

Use the worksheet below to create a wish list of items that you will need for your party planning experience. Use this when hiring a designer as a reference for the items that you would like as party décor.

NO. OF GUESTS _______________________________

THEME _______________________________

DECORATIONS
- [ ] Back Drop
- [ ] Arch (Balloon, flowers, etc)
- [ ] lighting
- [ ] banner
- [ ] easel (welcome sign)
- [ ] program (for table)
- [ ] champagne wall

TABLE SETTING
- [ ] plates - dinner, salad, dessert
- [ ] utensils - salad fork
- [ ] utensils - dinner fork
- [ ] utensils - spoon
- [ ] utensils - knife
- [ ] centerpieces
- [ ] charger
- [ ] napkins
- [ ] tableclothes

AREAS
- [ ] doorway
- [ ] front door
- [ ] stairway
- [ ] window seals
- [ ] cake /dessert display

____

- [ ] _______________________________
- [ ] _______________________________
- [ ] _______________________________
- [ ] _______________________________
- [ ] _______________________________
- [ ] _______________________________
- [ ] _______________________________
- [ ] _______________________________
- [ ] _______________________________
- [ ] _______________________________
- [ ] _______________________________
- [ ] _______________________________
- [ ] _______________________________
- [ ] _______________________________
- [ ] _______________________________
- [ ] _______________________________
- [ ] _______________________________

THE VAN/TRUCK RENTAL EXPERIENCE

Use the worksheet below to write down the names of truck rental companies that you plan to call or email.
- Once you have made a choice of which rental companies to call, collect needed information below
- Recommendations: U-Haul (van); You will need bungee cords and a hand truck)
- U-Haul will send information to your phone to confirm the reservation.

	INFORMATION
PRICE/QUOTE	
PHONE	
EMAIL	
NOTES	

PRICE/QUOTE	INFORMATION
PRICE/QUOTE	
PHONE	
EMAIL	
NOTES	

THE PARTY ITEMS RENTAL EXPERIENCE

Use the worksheet below to write down the names of party rental venues that you plan to call or email.

- Once you have made a choice of which rental companies to call, collect needed information below
- Ask questions that you may have about their timeline, types of set up for your venue, appointments to look at the venue, etc.
- Get a contact name, contract, sign it and place it in your party planning experience portfolio.
- Connect with the decorator as you get closer to the event date to confirm your date, timeline and final payment arrangements.

NO. OF GUESTS _______________

	COST ESTIMATE
PRICE/QUOTE	
PHONE	
EMAIL	
NOTES	

PARTY RENTALS	COST ESTIMATE
PRICE/QUOTE	
PHONE	
EMAIL	
NOTES	

RENTAL/PURCHASE LIST

Use the worksheet below to create a wish list of items that you will need for you party planning experience. Check all the items that you think that you will need for your venue. Some items will be purchased and some will be rented.

NO. OF GUESTS ______________________________

BAR AREA

- ☐ table or portable bar
- ☐ table cloth

CAKE AREA

- ☐ table
- ☐ table cloth
- ☐ knife and server
- ☐ pedestals

COCKTAIL AREA

- ☐ pedestal tables
- ☐ table clothes

ELECTRICAL TECHNOLOGY

- ☐ Audio Visual Equipment
- ☐ lighting

DISC JOCKEY

- ☐ table (if he/she does not have one)
- ☐ table cloth
- ☐ dance floor

FAVOR TABLE

- ☐ table
- ☐ table cloth
- ☐ favors

GIFT AREA

- ☐ table
- ☐ table cloth
- ☐ gift card box

GUEST TABLES

- ☐ tables
- ☐ table clothes
- ☐ napkins
- ☐ dinner, salad, bread plate
- ☐ chairs
- ☐ chairs covers
- ☐ water/tea glass
- ☐ fork, salad fork, knife, spoon

LOUNGE FURNITURE

- ☐ sofa
- ☐ chairs
- ☐ side tables
- ☐ coffee table

TENTING (they come in many sizes)

- ☐ 10 X 10
- ☐ 20 X 20
- ☐ 50 X 100

- ☐ ______________________
- ☐ ______________________
- ☐ ______________________
- ☐ ______________________

RENTAL/PURCHASE LIST

ITEM(S)	HOW MANY?	COST

06 | THE HOTEL ACCOMMODATIONS EXPERIENCE

Use the worksheet below to write down the names of hotels near you or the venue that you plan to call or email. It's best to let guest stay in a comfortable space so that they are not interrupting the party planning process. It is hard to focus when you have to entertain guest while planning for a party.

- Once you have made a hotel choice gather the information to send to your guest. (hotel name and address)
- Make sure that it is moderately priced for all guest
- Get the names of two moderately priced hotels and send it in text form (create an extra page connected to your invitation with the same format and color scheme)
- Send a reminder two weeks before the event to make sure that everyone has accommodations

HOTEL	INFORMATION
PRICE/QUOTE	
PHONE	
EMAIL	
NOTES	

HOTEL	INFORMATION
PRICE/QUOTE	
PHONE	
EMAIL	
NOTES	

07

DIGITAL
CORRESPONDENCE

Many people today have decided to go green and use the option of digital correspondence to communicate with their guest. This digital correspondence includes: save-the-dates, invitations, directions, table numbers, etc. It is easy to accomplish if you are tech savvy and know how to use creative software like Canva. You have an array of options to choose from so lets get started.

Technology is changing daily and their are many apps that assist with this process. Please feel free to research social media and other internet sources for the most updated apps available to make this job a smoother transition.

07
DIGITAL CORRESPONDENCE
SAVE-THE-DATE

For the past two decades, save the date cards have been very popular. This gives those people that you would like to invite a chance to plan for that special day.

You will need to choose a design that connects with the theme of your party (color and artwork). Canva is a great place to start this process. If you are not tech savvy, ask one of your friends to assist. There are instructions on how to create and send these digital products through text messaging on this page.

WHAT YOU WILL NEED . . .
- Color scheme and theme
- date of your event
- name of honoree
- guest list sheet

INSTRUCTIONS FOR CREATING THE DIGITAL STATIONERY
- Create the stationery (save-the-date) and download it to your computer
- Due to the swift nature of how technology changes daily, we keep an updated list of instructions on how to modify the free products we offer on our website for you to download and follow.
- Go to: www.thepartyplanningexperience.com/free-resources
- You do not need an RSVP for a save-the-date
- You may also visit some of the online websites and apps that have digital products

INSTRUCTIONS FOR SENDING DIGITAL STATIONERY
- Create the stationery (save-the-date) and download it as a png. file to your computer
- Open your email and attach the save-the-date and send it to your email
- Open the email on your phone and download the attachment to your camera roll
- You will now be able to send this to each of your guest as a text message

07
DIGITAL CORRESPONDENCE INVITATION

Once you have let everyone know about your plans for the event you can begin to plan for invitation selection. It is best to create a digital invitation to save time and money. You will choose an invitation that "speaks" to everyone when they open their text. It should get everyone excited about the theme of your event. This can be created on Canva. There are instructions below on how to send an invitation by text messaging .

You will need to choose a design that connects with the theme of your party (color and artwork). Canva is a great place to start this process. If you are not tech savvy, ask one of your friends to assist.

WHAT YOU WILL NEED . . .
- Color scheme and theme
- date of your event
- place of event
- name of honoree
- guest list sheet
- digital invitation

INSTRUCTIONS FOR CREATING THE DIGITAL STATIONERY
- Create the stationery (invitation) and download it as a png. file to your computer
- Due to the swift nature of how technology changes daily, we keep an updated list of instructions on how to modify the free products we offer on our website for you to download and follow.
- Go to: www.thepartyplanningexperience.com/free-resources
- You may also visit some of the online websites and apps that have digital products

INSTRUCTIONS FOR SENDING THE DIGITAL STATIONERY
- Create the stationery (invitation) and download it as a png. file to your computer
- Open your email and attach the save-the-date and send it to your email
- Open the email on your phone and download the attachment to your camera roll
- You will now be able to send this to each of your guest as a text message

07
PRINT CORRESPONDENCE INVITATION

If you have chosen to create a paper invitation it is a great way to communicate your event with "class". You will choose an invitation that "speaks" to your event. When your guest receive it in the mail the color, paper texture and artwork will get them excited about the event. You will need to choose a design that connects with the theme of your party.

WHAT YOU WILL NEED . . .
- Color scheme and theme
- date of your event
- place of event
- Time (beginning and ending)
- name of honoree(s)
- rsvp (yes/no) make a QR code to place on the card that will go to a website or Google form
- guest list sheet with names and addresses (look in the back of this book for resources on how to create this form)

INSTRUCTIONS FOR CREATING THE PAPER INVITATION
- You will need to use an online platform to make the invitation and have it printed.
- We recommend Canva or Vista Print
- If you use Canva you may also visit your local print shop (i.e. Staples, FedEx Office)
- You will need to be tech savvy to create this project (get a friend to help)

INSTRUCTIONS FOR SENDING THE PAPER INVITATION
- Create mailing labels (return address and guest address)
- Purchase stamps that connect with your theme
- If you used an online printer, proofread your invitations when they arrive to make sure that all of the information is correct. Mail them 30-45 days before the event.

07

DIGITAL CORRESPONDENCE
TABLE NUMBERS

This task is designed for party planners expecting over 40 guests who need to maintain organization. Table numbers should be printed and placed on the tables, possibly in frames. To streamline guest logistics and help them find their assigned seats, consider texting guests their table numbers two days before the event.

There is a folder in the download document that you received that has a set of numbers that you can download to your phone and send to guests. If you are tech savvy you can use Canva and create numbers that match your theme. Follow the instruction below for sending digital stationery.

WHAT YOU WILL NEED . . .
- Color scheme and theme
- table numbers
- guest list sheet
- digital invitation (png version) 4" x 6"

INSTRUCTIONS FOR SENDING DIGITAL STATIONERY
- Create the stationery (table number) or download the one given in your package
- Download it as a png. file to your computer
- Open your email and attach the table number and send it to your email
- Open the email on your phone and download the attachment to your camera roll
- You will now be able to send this to each of your guest as a text message (Please see the example text message of verbiage that needs to be added with this document on the text verbiage page)

DIGITAL CORRESPONDENCE
SIGNAGE

There are signs that you can create to enhance your party. These signs will direct guests, share important information, and/or add a decorative touch. Below is a list of commonly used signs. Get them printed at you local print shop. This will make them look professional. Paste them on form board or put them in a frame. Get little clear plastic stands from the discount store. This would be a good time to use contingency fund!

WELCOME SIGN
- A sign at the entrance greeting guests

SEATING CHART (NEEDED FOR MORE THAN 40 PPL)
- Showing guests where to find their tables

GIFT TABLE SIGN
- Directing guests where to place their gifts.

BAR MENU/SIGN
- List of available drinks or special cocktails that are prepared for your guest enjoyment.

HASHTAG SIGN
- Encouraging guests to use a specific hashtag for social media so that you can find those special photos #sargeantwedding2017.

PRINTING

DIY PRINTING
- Create your own signage using Canva or a Word Document. Browse the internet for a beautiful font and look for a style that matches your theme. If you would like to make it look professional go to your local Staples or FedEx Office and print them on cardstock. You can always add ribbon or greenery for a decorative touch.

07

DIGITAL CORRESPONDENCE
TEXT PHRASEOLOGY

Use this as a guide and change it to fit your particular event. You will need to have language to go along with your correspondence so that guests understand how to respond. Read the examples below.

SAVE THE DATE
- I am sending this SAVE-THE-DATE so that you can make plans to attend our mother's 60th birthday. Please respond yes by January 1
- Shh! It's a surprise. I am sending this SAVE-THE-DATE so that you can make plans to attend our mother's 60th birthday. Please respond yes by January 1.

INVITATION
- We are so excited that you decided to join us on this special occasion. The attire is connected with dad's favorite football team. Please wear black and gold. This is a very special adult affair. (It's ok to say that no children are allowed). Please respond yes by February 1.

PARTY REMINDER
- Don't forget about the party tomorrow. Cocktail hour will begin promptly at 5:00pm and dinner will be served at 6:00pm. We are so happy that you decided to join us. The weather is going to be warm at 80 degrees with clear skies. Let's get ready to party!

SEATING CHART/TABLE NUMBERS (MORE THAN 40 PPL)
- We are honored that you decided to join us on February 28 for the surprise birthday party. You will be sitting at .... (You will text the table number)

THANK YOU
- Thank you so much for making this surprise party a great success. I will be sure to keep you on the party list!
- Thank you for attending our Valentine's Day Celebration. You bought so much love and energy to this event. See you next time.

CHAPTER 08

THE ENTERTAINMENT

The importance of music for your guests' party experience cannot be overstated, as it serves as the heartbeat of the event, setting the tone and shaping the overall ambiance. Music has a profound effect on mood and emotions, and selecting the right playlist or live performance can greatly enhance the atmosphere and create lasting memories for attendees. Whether it's a lively dance floor filled with upbeat tunes or a laid-back gathering accompanied by soothing melodies, the choice of music directly impacts how guests engage with the event and each other. The rhythmic beats and melodic harmonies of well-curated music have the power to uplift spirits, evoke nostalgia, and foster a sense of connection and community among attendees, making it a fundamental element of any successful party.

Moreover, music serves as a universal language that transcends cultural barriers and brings people together in celebration and joy. Regardless of age, background, or preferences, guests can find common ground and shared enjoyment through the shared experience of music. From sing-alongs to spontaneous dance-offs, music provides a platform for guests to express themselves freely and connect with others in meaningful ways. By curating a diverse and inclusive playlist that appeals to a wide range of tastes and preferences, hosts can ensure that every guest feels welcomed and included, contributing to a positive and memorable party experience for all.

The music for your event will set the tone and mood of how your guest feel during your party experience. From the time that they come into your chosen venue their senses will be stimulated with the sounds of familiar melodies. Invite them to come in a get a drink, relax and listen to the entertainment.

LIVE

The joy given from a live band at a party is unparalleled, as their dynamic presence adds an infectious energy that elevates the atmosphere and creates a memorable experience for guests. With the ability to adapt their repertoire to suit the mood of the event, live bands engage attendees on a personal level, fostering a sense of connection and shared enjoyment. Their authentic performance and skillful musicianship create a captivating ambiance that encourages participation and leaves a lasting impression.

SOLO

The performance of a solo musician accompanied by digital music at a party is equally remarkable, as their performance brings the unique sound of live talent. They usually play a clarinet, flute, or keyboard accompanied with digital sounds sound to infused the space with a captivating energy that keep your guests engage in the atmosphere of the moment. This dynamic combination allows for versatility in genre and style, ensuring that the music resonates with the mood of the event and the preferences of the audience.

DJ

A DJ brings an unparalleled level of versatility and excitement to the event, effortlessly transitioning between songs and genres to keep the energy high and the dance floor packed. When you choose a DJ for your party experience you want one who has the expertise to read the crowd and select the perfect tracks. A good DJ also creates a personalized and dynamic musical experience that resonates with guests of all ages and tastes. Go online and find a video of your favorite DJ. Most of them have had someone record some of their events.

DIGITAL

Using a digital form of entertainment is not a bad thing these days. Depending on your party level you may not need to spend the funds for a vendor. In this case you can opt to create a playlist on on of the online platforms like Spotify, Google Play, Apple Music and the like. You should create several playlist based on your theme, age group, and timeline for your event. Most parties begin with smooth sounds and gradually grow to more upbeat rhythms. Create at least three playlist for this timeline and use a Bluetooth speaker to "blast the night away."

08 | THE LIVE MUSIC EXPERIENCE

Use the worksheet below to write down the names of live bands that you plan to call or email. Take a look at some of the online platforms that list bands and singers for hire.

- Once you have made a choice on which bands to call, collect needed information below
- Ask questions the timeline that they need for set up or if they are familiar with your venue.
- Get a contact name, contract, sign it and place it in your party planning experience portfolio.
- Connect with the band as you get closer to the event date to confirm your date, timeline and final payment arrangements.

LIVE MUSIC	INFORMATION
PRICE/QUOTE	
PHONE	
EMAIL	
NOTES	

LIVE MUSIC	INFORMATION
PRICE/QUOTE	
PHONE	
EMAIL	
NOTES	

08 | THE SOLO MUSICIAN EXPERIENCE

Use the worksheet below to write down the names of solo musician artist that you plan to call or email. Take a look at some of the online platforms that list solo musician for hire.

- Once you have made a choice on which artist to call, collect needed information below
- Ask questions the timeline that they need for set up or if they are familiar with your venue.
- Get a contact name, contract, sign it and place it in your party planning experience portfolio.
- Connect with the artist as you get closer to the event date to confirm your date, timeline and final payment arrangements.

SOLO ARTIST	INFORMATION
PRICE/QUOTE	
PHONE	
EMAIL	
NOTES	

SOLO ARTIST	INFORMATION
PRICE/QUOTE	
PHONE	
EMAIL	
NOTES	

08 | THE DISC JOCKEY EXPERIENCE

Use the worksheet below to write down the names of a DJ that you plan to call or email.
Take a look at some of the online platforms that list disc jockeys and singers for hire.

- Once you have made a choice on which DJ to call, collect needed information below
- Ask questions the timeline that they need for set up or if they are familiar with your venue.
- Get a contact name, contract, sign it and place it in your party planning experience portfolio.
- Connect with the DJ as you get closer to the event date to confirm your date, timeline and final payment arrangements.

DISC JOCKEY	INFORMATION
PRICE/QUOTE	
PHONE	
EMAIL	
NOTES	

DISC JOCKEY	INFORMATION
PRICE/QUOTE	
PHONE	
EMAIL	
NOTES	

08 | THE DIGITAL MUSIC EXPERIENCE

This information will assist you with getting your digital music organized for your special event.

- You will begin to create music playlist for your event on your platform of choice, based on the genre that connects with the taste of your guest (mellow music, slow music, dance music)
- If you have Spotify there is a starter list of songs on www.thepartyplanningexperience.com/music
- Listen to these playlist while in the car and around the house to make sure that the songs are right for you.
- You may create new playlist (Example: Pop Songs, R & B songs, etc)
- TIP: If you borrow a Bluetooth speaker make sure it has all of the parts when you pick it up. Make sure that to pick it up early enough to learn the system and how you will connect it to your phone's system.

DIGITAL MUSIC ITEMS

- bluetooth speaker
- long extension cord
- playlist (one for each segment of your event)
- microphone (some speakers have a microphone jack)

08 | THE ENTERTAINMENT EXPERIENCE

Add an extra layer of joy to your event by adding interactive entertainment. If you have few dollars to splurge or if a friend would like to gift you their talent choose one of the items below. Your guests will love you.

NO OF GUESTS _______________________________

THEME _______________________________

- [ ] beer pong
- [ ] caricature artist
- [ ] cigar bar
- [ ] comedy show
- [ ] hookah lounge
- [ ] karaoke
- [ ] photo booth 360 cell phone video
- [ ] scavenger hunt

08 | THE CIGAR LOUNGE EXPERIENCE

Use the worksheet below to write down the names of mobile cigar company that you plan to call or email.

- Once you have made a choice on which mobile cigar company to call, collect needed information below
- Ask questions the timeline that they need for set up or if they are familiar with your venue.
- Get a contact name, contract, sign it and place it in your party planning experience portfolio.
- Connect with the cigar company as you get closer to the event date to confirm your date, timeline and final payment arrangements.

CIGAR LOUNGE	INFORMATION
PRICE/QUOTE	
PHONE	
EMAIL	
NOTES	

CIGAR LOUNGE	INFORMATION
PRICE/QUOTE	
PHONE	
EMAIL	
NOTES	

08 | THE HOOKAH LOUNGE EXPERIENCE

Use the worksheet below to write down the names of mobile hookah businesses that you plan to call or email.

- Once you have made a choice on which business to call, collect needed information below
- Ask questions the timeline that they need for set up or if they are familiar with your venue.
- Get a contact name, contract, sign it and place it in your party planning experience portfolio.
- Connect with the mobile hookah lounge business as you get closer to the event date to confirm your date, timeline and final payment arrangements.

HOOKAH LOUNGE	INFORMATION
PRICE/QUOTE	
PHONE	
EMAIL	
NOTES	

HOOKAH LOUNGE	INFORMATION
PRICE/QUOTE	
PHONE	
EMAIL	
NOTES	

08 | THE PHOTOGRAPHY EXPERIENCE

Use the worksheet below to write down the names of photographers that you plan to call or email.

- How many hours will you need the photographer? _______
- What time will you need the photographer at the venue? _______
- Try to find a recommendation from a friend, someone who is starting their business, or someone you know who has a good camera. This is not a wedding so you don't need to pay wedding prices.
- Write down questions you may have about the service.
- Get a contract, signed it and place it in your party planning experience portfolio.
- Connect with the photographer as you get closer to the event date to confirm your date, time of deliveries and payment arrangements.

PHOTOGRAPHER	INFORMATION
PRICE/QUOTE	
PHONE	
EMAIL	
NOTES	

PHOTOGRAPHER	INFORMATION
PRICE/QUOTE	
PHONE	
EMAIL	
NOTES	

LET'S GET READY TO PARTY!

This is the part of the timeline that can become stressful if you have not planned and paced tasks along the way. But fear not, you can "phone a friend." Utilize the "1-hour" free consultation provided with the purchase of this guide for assistance with last-minute planning. Think about having a day planner on hand (hired or family). This person is not just an expense, but a strategic ally in orchestrating a successful party. They serve as a compass, guiding you through the intricate web of preparations, ensuring no detail is overlooked or left to chance. After meeting with them, they will have a good grasp of how to transform the chaotic jumble of ideas and follow the timeline, delineating tasks with clarity and purpose. The day planner becomes a repository of vision, capturing the essence of the event and translating it into actionable steps. Beyond its organizational prowess, a day planner is a shield against forgetfulness and last-minute tasks. In essence, it is the cornerstone of a well-executed affair, embodying the adage that "by failing to prepare, you are preparing to fail."

DAY BEFORE SCHEDULE

This is a sample "day before the party" schedule for a Saturday event that takes place at 6:00pm and runs for 4 hours to 10:00pm. You should take leave from work to plan the day before

8:00 am
- charge your phone
- meditate or say a prayer
- go over your plan for the day

9:00 am
- hydrate and eat light breakfast
- gather your checklist (check once, check twice)
- lay out your outfit (s)

10:00 am
- hair appointment

11:00 am

12:00 n
- have lunch and relax

1:00 pm
- send a party reminder (see correspondence chapter)

2:00 pm
- nail salon appointment

3:00 pm
- pickup U-haul van if needed

4:00 pm
- confirm helpers
- confirm day of planner
- confirm vendors

5:00 pm

6:00 pm
- pack your car or truck (lock the door)
- Check that everything is in place

7:00 pm
- continue gathering items need for tomorrow's event and place near the door so that you won't forget them

DAY BEFORE SCHEDULE

8:00 am _______________________

9:00 am _______________________

10:00 am _______________________

11:00 am _______________________

12:00 n _______________________

1:00 pm _______________________

2:00 pm _______________________

3:00 pm _______________________

4:00 pm _______________________

5:00 pm _______________________

6:00 pm _______________________

7:00 pm _______________________

This is a sample party schedule is for a Saturday event that takes place at 6:00pm and runs for 4 hours to 10:00pm.

8:00 am

- charge you phone
- meditate or say a prayer
- go over you plan for the day

9:00 am

- hydrate and eat light breakfast
- lay out your outfit (s)

10:00 am

- pack last minute items in the car, van, truck

11:00 am

- confirm all vendors and orders

12:00 n

1:00 pm

2:00 pm

- Relax
- Start getting dress

3:00 pm

4:00 pm

- Leave home or hotel to go to the party

5:00 pm

- Arrive at venue to begin to greet guest
- Check that everything is in place
- Make sure music is playing to set the mood

6:00 pm

- Cocktail Hour
- Make an introduction of the party

7:00 pm

- Dinner Hour
- (7:45) Presentations, Congratulations, Speakers,

DAY OF SCHEDULE

8:00 pm

- Cut cake, serve dessert or ice cream

9:00 pm

- Dance the night away

10:00 pm

- Start clean up

DAY OF SCHEDULE

8:00 am _______________________

9:00 am _______________________

10:00 am _______________________

11:00 am _______________________

12:00 n _______________________

1:00 pm _______________________

2:00 pm _______________________

3:00 pm _______________________

4:00 pm _______________________

5:00 pm _______________________

6:00 pm _______________________

7:00 pm _______________________

DAY OF SCHEDULE

8:00 pm _______________________

9:00 pm _______________________

10:00 pm ______________________

Use this list of assignments to give to the assistant(s) or family members so that they have a defined list of duties. Use the blank sheet on the next page to complete for each assistant.

ATTIRE

- The assistant(s) should be dressed in black pants, black shoes and a white pressed shirt. If they need assistance with attire and you want to make sure they are dressed appropriately you can purchase a shirt from the thrift store or Amazon. It's important to look professional.

BAR

- Take all items out of the bags and set up the bar station
- greet guest "how may I help you" or "what would like to order"
- place ice in glass if requested and a garnish on each glass
- keep the area clean
- notify the host early if the ice is running low

DECOR

- Take all items out of the bags and place on the table
- This can be a two person task. One person should be assigned to complete one task at a time (place table clothes on table)
- place all table clothes on first, then centerpieces, chargers, plates, utensils, stemware, butter, salt and pepper (in that order)
- They can assist with various decorations if you did not hire a designer (props, streamers, balloons)

COATS

- This task is for cold season events. You will need: coat rack and numbered tags (purchase "live sales numbers from Amazon)
- Have the numbers in order (1, 2, 3....) Take guests coats and hang them on a hanger and let them take a picture of the number. When they return, they will be able to find their coat quickly.

CLEAN UP

- Take items off of the table as guest finish each course, salad, dinner and dessert plates. Throw away drink cups that are unattended.
- check bathroom at the top of each hour for tidiness, and to fill tissue
- change trash bags periodically

ASSISTANT SCHEDULE

NAME

BAR

DECOR

COATS

CLEAN UP

09 DAY OF PLANNER

TIME	ACTIVITY

THE RESOURCES

This section is comprised of extra resources and tips that you will need to make you event a success.

RESOURCES

GENTLY USED
- Facebook Marketplace - You need to be a Facebook user to use this source)
- Goodwill Retail Store
- Salvation Army Family Store
- Thrift Stores - (Some areas of the US have charity thrift stores - hospitals, and nonprofits "Google It")
- Yard sales

ONLINE
- Ali Express
- Amazon
- Ebay
- Efavormart
- Etsy
- Ling's Moments
- Petal Garden
- Save on Crafts
- Shop Wild Things
- Temu
- Totally Dazzled

STORES
- A.C. Moore Arts and Crafts
- At Home (Not Everywhere - Check the website)
- Hobby Lobby
- Michael's
- Paper Source
- Staples
- Your locally owned party stores

DIGITAL/ONLINE
- Apple Music
- Canva - Use for signage and other print needs
- iHeart Radio
- Pandora
- Spotify - Go to www.thepartyplanningexperience.com and click on the music page playlist. We have created list for you!
- Vista Print

FREE!
1 hour Consultation
You must text to set up an appointment
703-609-2152
"Hi my name is __________. I just purchased your party planning guide and would like to get my free 1 hour consultation."

GETTING READY
FOR
THE PARTY

- Rent a U-Haul van or truck to move items needed for the party. U-Haul vans rent for $19.00 a day. Pick it up the day before.
- purchase plastic containers and use a small cart with wheels (or hand truck from U-Haul) to move heavy items.
- pack all of your items in a container and place near the door
- purchase a plastic shoe box from the discount store to place small items inside so that you can find them (place packing tape on each end so that items do not spill out during travel)
- if the space does not have a bar area you will need the suggested 6ft table and a black stretch tablecloth (order this from Amazon early)
- If you some of guest need to bring children prepare a children's corner with crayons, coloring sheets and Legos.
- if it is winter time you will need a "coat check" area. Purchase huggable hangers and "live sale numbers" from Amazon to place on coats. Use one of those portable coat racks.
- if you are getting mylar balloons you can get them the day before
- If you are hosting the party at home, set up things the night before
- send your guest a hotel accommodations reminder two weeks before the event
- If hosting the party at home, clear all items off of the counter top to set up buffet. Make sure that you have toilet paper, poo-pourri spray and small napkins in the restroom (use cocktail size)
- Visit YouTube to get cake cutting instructions. The general rule is 1" wide by 2" deep.
- Purchase small bottles of water to give to guest as they leave to help them stay awake on the drive home
- Sam's creates theme cakes and they are inexpensive two-tier cakes starting at $41.00
- If you are in a budget crunch and need to think about a catering idea that is elegant and inexpensive, use one of the menus provided in this guide to create a tasty meal
- Order decorations as soon as you have secured your venue
- purchase a broom and mop from the Dollar Tree to clean up spills if you are at an outside venue
- Home Depot sells a portable trash can that uses 13 gal. trash bags.
- Bring plastic zip bags and containers to pack leftovers.
- Bring foil to wrap the cake

10 IN PROCESS

FINAL PARTY CHECKLIST

DECORATIONS

- [ ] __________________________
- [ ] __________________________
- [ ] __________________________
- [ ] __________________________
- [ ] __________________________
- [ ] __________________________
- [ ] __________________________
- [ ] __________________________
- [ ] __________________________
- [ ] __________________________
- [ ] __________________________
- [ ] __________________________
- [ ] __________________________
- [ ] __________________________
- [ ] __________________________

BAR

- [ ] __________________________
- [ ] __________________________
- [ ] __________________________
- [ ] __________________________
- [ ] __________________________
- [ ] __________________________
- [ ] __________________________
- [ ] __________________________
- [ ] __________________________
- [ ] __________________________
- [ ] __________________________
- [ ] __________________________
- [ ] __________________________
- [ ] __________________________
- [ ] __________________________

CATERING

- [ ] __________________________
- [ ] __________________________
- [ ] __________________________
- [ ] __________________________
- [ ] __________________________
- [ ] __________________________
- [ ] __________________________
- [ ] __________________________
- [ ] __________________________
- [ ] __________________________
- [ ] __________________________
- [ ] __________________________
- [ ] __________________________
- [ ] __________________________
- [ ] __________________________

VENDORS

- [ ] __________________________
- [ ] __________________________
- [ ] __________________________
- [ ] __________________________
- [ ] __________________________
- [ ] __________________________
- [ ] __________________________
- [ ] __________________________
- [ ] __________________________
- [ ] __________________________
- [ ] __________________________
- [ ] __________________________
- [ ] __________________________
- [ ] __________________________
- [ ] __________________________

10 MASTER/MISTRESS OF CEREMONIES

Here's a template for the master/mistress of ceremonies (MC) to introduce the honor guest for which the party is being given, along with a section for others to say a few words, and an ending .

SAMPLE

Introduction of Honored Guest

Ladies and gentlemen, distinguished guests, and friends, welcome to this special occasion where we gather to celebrate [Name of Honored Guest]. Today/Tonight, we honor [him/her] for at this [brief reason for celebration, e.g., birthday, retirement, achievements, etc.].

[Optional: Share a brief anecdote or story about the guest to personalize the introduction.]

Please join me in welcoming and congratulating [Name of Honored Guest] on/at [his/her] [e.g., birthday, retirement, achievements, etc.] !

Story:
Tell something special about the person [family, job, hobbies, achievements, poem]
Invitation for Remarks:

At this time, we would like to offer the opportunity for anyone who wishes to share a few words or a special message for [Name of Honored Guest] to come forward. Whether you've known [him/her] for years or have a recent memory to share, we invite you to share your thoughts.

Ending to Transition to Dancing

As we've celebrated this milestone with [Name of Honored Guest], it's time to kick off the festivities! I invite everyone to join us on the dance floor as we continue the celebration with music, laughter, and joy. Let's make this a(n) [evening/night] to remember!

Feel free to customize this template as needed for your specific event and theme.

CATERING BUFFET SET-UP

ITEMS	SERVING DISH CONTAINER	UTENSILS

GIFT ACHKNOWLEDGEMENTS

NO.	ITEM	PERSON(S)

CREATE "GMAIL"

It is called Google Workspace. Creating a "Gmail" address is a straightforward process. Here are step-by-step instructions.
This "Google Workspace" will be used for family members to have access to digital information. You can used the Google Drive to hold documents that need to be shared by all. You can also scan and upload to the area. This email can be used for the doctor and other entities so that the information does not get confused with the personal email of the caretaker.

1. Open Your Browser
   Open your preferred web browser (e.g., Chrome, Firefox, Safari).

2. Go to Gmail
   Type "Gmail" into the search bar or go directly to the Gmail website by entering "gmail.com" in the address bar.

3. Create an Account
   Once on the Gmail homepage, look for the option that says "Create account" or "Sign up." Click on it.

4. Fill in the Information
   Enter your first and last name in the provided fields.
   Choose a unique username for your Gmail address. This will be the part of your email address before the "@" symbol. If the username is already taken, Gmail will suggest variations or you can choose a different one.
   Create a strong and secure password. Gmail will indicate the strength of your password as you type it. Make sure
   to use a combination of letters, numbers, and symbols.

username _________________________________   password _________________________________
(use something like sharonparty@gmail.com)

5. Confirm Password
   Retype your chosen password to confirm it.

6. Provide Additional Information
   Enter your phone number and recovery email address. This information is crucial for account recovery purposes.

7. Verify Your Identity
   Google may ask you to verify your identity by sending a verification code to your phone number or recovery email. Enter the code when prompted.

8. Agree to Terms and Conditions
   Read and accept Google's Terms of Service and Privacy Policy.

9. Complete Setup
   Follow any additional on-screen instructions to complete the setup process, such as adding a profile picture if desired.

10. Access Your Gmail
    Once the account creation process is complete, you can sign in to your new Gmail address using your username
    and password.

That's it! You've successfully created a Gmail address. Remember to keep your login credentials secure and consider setting up two-factor authentication for added security.

CREATE GUEST LIST FORM

It is called Google Workspace. After creating you "Gmail" you will have access to the Google Workspace. This next step will be easy and this form will give you control of the names and addresses. The guest will complete the form and the information will automatically populate into a spreadsheet.

OPEN YOUR BROWSER

SIGN INTO YOUR GMAIL

- Go to the apps in the right hand corner of the screen and click on the (9 black dots). Click on "Drive". When you open Drive look on the left side of the screen and click "new"; Google form; and blank form

Click on the "Blank form" option
- Modify the title of the form.

CREATE THE NVITATION FORM (please complete a section for each of these because this can be used for multiple things and you will be able to place the names in ABC order on the spreadsheet

CREATE A NEW SECTION FOR EACH OF THESE ITEMS
- Title (create a dropdown with Mr., Mrs., Ms., Dr., Drs., Honorable
- Last Name
- First Name
- Address
- City
- State
- Zip
- Phone
- email
- If you are not tech savvy enough to make this you will need help or go to YouTube and search "CREATE A GOOGLE FORM"
- This Google Form will capture this information and place it in a spreadsheet for you to manipulate during the event planning process.
- After creating this Google Form you will need to go to the little icon that looks like an "eye". Click on this to view the form. You will copy the link in the address bar and create a shorter version call a (bit.ly) link to send to invited guests through text. This is also a task that you may need assistance on. Go to YouTube and search "Create a bit.ly."
- Before sending the link, text your bestie to see if all things are working properly.
- If it is working, text this bit.ly link to people that you have listed on your guest list with the message below.

MESSAGE

Hi, this is _______________. I am collecting names and addresses for the birthday party so that I can mail formal invitations. Please complete the form by clicking on the link as soon as possible. Thank you.

THE PARYY

PLANNING EXPERIENCE

Thank you for purchasing "THE PARTY PLANNING EXPERIENCE" guide book. There are over 50 additional themed books coming soon to accompany this comprehensive guide. Please take a look at what we have available. Let's Get Ready To Party!

www.thepartyplanningexperience.com

BY SHARON SARGEANT